Original title:
The Journey to Finding Life's Meaning

Copyright © 2025 Creative Arts Management OÜ
All rights reserved.

Author: Julian Carmichael
ISBN HARDBACK: 978-1-80566-213-6
ISBN PAPERBACK: 978-1-80566-508-3

Secrets Hidden in Sunlight

I walked outside, thought I was wise,
But tripped on a shoe, much to my surprise.
The sun laughed bright, said, "That's quite a jest!"
"Just enjoy your fall; you're still the best!"

With shadows dancing, trying to tease,
I chased them all day with the greatest of ease.
But shadows don't laugh, they just like to hide,
So I ended up lost, with nowhere to glide.

Harvesting the Colors of Life

I picked a red apple, it winked with delight,
Said, "Eat me with cheese! It's a culinary fight!"
Then oranges chimed in, full of zest,
Claiming the title of fruit-fighting best!

Bananas just laughed, swinging on trees,
"We're the comedians, eat us if you please!"
Life's fruity debate, so silly and bright,
In a world full of colors, I took a big bite!

The Tides of Contemplation

On the beach I sat, the waves came to play,
They whispered sweet secrets that washed me away.
"What's the meaning?" I asked with a frown,
The seagulls just cackled and turned right around.

The tide tried to answer with a splash of foam,
But all it did was send my thoughts home.
With a nod and a grin, I floated along,
Life's questions are silly and that's where I belong!

Unseen Threads of Existence

I wore mismatched socks, thought I was clever,
But lost one today, well, that's just my endeavor.
The laundry spun tales of a sock on the roam,
"Finding true meaning? You're stuck here at home!"

With threads all a-tangle, I stitched up my fate,
"You can't wear them both! They just won't correlate!"
In the fabric of life, I stumbled and sighed,
But laughed as I realized, it's a whimsical ride!

The Voice Beneath the Noise

In a world where chaos reigns,
I ask for signs, like traffic lanes.
The pigeons coo, the honkers blare,
Yet I just want a moment spare.

I lost my keys inside a sock,
Is that the wisdom of the clock?
The mailman laughs, my lunch is gone,
I nod my head, keep moving on.

The coffee spills, my shirt's a mess,
I find life's truths in such distress.
The world out there might seem a race,
But humor is my saving grace.

So here I stand, a curious chap,
With goofy thoughts upon my map.
A smile shared, a silly joke,
Turns heavy loads to light and smoke.

Sketches of a Soul's Expedition

I packed my bags with cheer and glee,
  Forgot my socks, but found a bee.
With quips and quarks, I start to roam,
An awkward dance that feels like home.

  The map I drew led me astray,
    I ended up in a cabaret.
  The jester jigs, I trip and spin,
Life's just a laugh, let the fun begin.

I wander through a field of trees,
Chasing squirrels who tease with ease.
Each nut a lesson, quite absurd,
  In nutty wisdom, I find my word.

So sketch a life that bends and sways,
  With quirky tales of oddball days.
For meaning hides in laughter's light,
  With every giggle, I take a flight.

The Color of Transcendence

I painted dreams in boldest hues,
Mixed mustard yellow with my blues.
A rainbow spritz on drab gray walls,
Where laughter's echo endlessly calls.

With crayons sharp, I doodled fate,
A cat on skates, a dancing plate.
While wisdom whispers in a grin,
Life's colorful chaos pulls me in.

I tripped on paint, then looked around,
Where every stumble brought new ground.
With brush in hand, I daubed a grin,
In the mess, my truths begin.

So splash a canvas, bright and bold,
In colors rich, let stories unfold.
For meaning's found in strokes of fun,
In each wild swirl, we're all just one.

Climbing the Mountains of Thought

I strapped my shoes, began to climb,
With every step, I lost some time.
My mind a jumble, thoughts like sheep,
Where's that mountain? I need some sleep.

I slipped on rocks, did a silly dance,
My brain's a circus, never chance.
Yet every stutter, every fall,
Has drawn a map upon the wall.

I met a sage who sells ice cream,
He said, "Kid, life's not what it seems."
So I took a scoop, we laughed aloud,
I shouted back, "I'm feeling proud!"

With every peak, I shed a fear,
The view's quite nice from up here, my dear.
So climb those peaks, take silly routes,
In your heart's laughs, life's meaning sprouts.

A Tapestry of Trials

I sought the truth in cookie crumbs,
But realized they're just for tums.
I chased the meaning in a song,
Only to find I sang it wrong.

With maps that lead to nowhere fast,
I packed my bags but forgot the past.
I wandered through a field of socks,
And wondered why they talked like rocks.

I tripped on paths that made me grin,
Insurance claims are quite a win.
I pondered deep with wooden spoons,
And argued with the marching loons.

In every left and every right,
I found the flaws that brought delight.
So here's to life with all its jests,
A tapestry of quirky quests.

Songs of the Unseen Traveler

A traveler humming like a bee,
Sang tunes about lack of glee.
His suitcase full of mismatched shoes,
He danced away all of his blues.

He crossed a bridge of soggy bread,
And claimed that dreams were made of thread.
With every step and silly pout,
He learned what life was really about.

He asked the sun for tips on smiles,
And got lost in the moon's sweet wiles.
With laughter ringing like soft bells,
He found the joy in all life spells.

Together with the trees he sang,
While nature nodded and just rang.
The unseen traveler with a grin,
Found meaning deep in all the din.

Lanterns of Hope

With a lantern lit by fireflies,
I trekked the world, ignoring sighs.
I stumbled on a puddle wide,
And in it saw my dreamy ride.

A wandering gnome with silly jokes,
Shared secrets of the honest folks.
He said, "Just find a pie to bake,
And life will give you many a break."

I juggled dreams like bowling balls,
And answered nature's quirky calls.
What lies ahead? Who really knows?
A garden where the laughter grows.

With each bright flicker of my light,
I danced into the wild delight.
Lanterns shone and hope awoke,
As chuckles filled the air with smoke.

When Stars Align

When stars align, or so they say,
I found my socks were on the sway.
With pizza slices flying high,
I chased the cheese across the sky.

My alarm clock rang with silly tunes,
As I asked the sun for more cartoons.
With coffee spills and laughter loud,
I planned my journey past the crowd.

A talking cat claimed he knew best,
But napped through all my crazy quests.
A map made of jelly and a whisk,
Showed paths where caffeine is the risk.

So here I am with doodles bright,
Beneath the stars, I chase delight.
When dreams align, just grab a slice,
Life's meaning hides in fun and spice.

A Dance of Possibilities

In a world of mismatched socks,
I twirl, I spin, avoiding clocks.
With pancake hats and shoes askew,
Life's silly dance is all I rue.

I try to find a noble quest,
But end up napping, that's the best!
For wisdom hides in simple things,
Like rubber ducks with tiny wings.

I ponder deeply while I snack,
On bowls of chips, I can't look back.
Each crunch reveals a thought or two,
Or something sticky on my shoe.

Yet through the giggles and the falls,
I learn to hear the laughter calls.
In bubbles blown, and silly tunes,
Life's meaning drifts like paper moons.

Sails of Solitude

I set my sails on a paper boat,
With ice cream dreams and notes that float.
The wind is strong—it's just my breath,
But donuts cheer me, conquering death.

On waves of crumbs, I surf with glee,
The jellyfish sing, they laugh with me.
Finding treasure in what I eat,
A sandwich map with cookies sweet.

When solitude knocks, I dance by myself,
To kooky tunes from the bookcase shelf.
A solo act with shoes so bright,
I wobble, giggle, and take flight.

Each "ahoy!" I boldly declare,
To seagulls who don't seem to care.
In this quiet ride—how absurd!
The meaning floats on every bird.

Threads of Fate Weaved Together

I stitched my thoughts with frayed old yarn,
A tapestry bright, yet somewhat worn.
Each knot a joke, each fringe a laugh,
As I unravel the world's own path.

With needles made from candy cane,
I sew my dreams in every stain.
Just watch me weave my wild delight,
Beneath the stars that twinkle bright.

I tug and pull at tangled threads,
A wardrobe full of silly spreads.
While fate may tangle, twist and twine,
I dress in colors, bold, divine.

What meaning lies in fabric fine?
A patchwork heart, a goofy sign.
In every stitch, a memory twirls,
Life's fabric dances, swirls and whirls.

Beneath the Surface of Serenity

In ponds of giggles, frogs wear crowns,
Where laughter bubbles, no room for frowns.
I dive beneath, in silly quests,
To find the calm in playful jests.

With waves of ripples, I splash around,
A synchronized swim without a sound.
Each bubble pops, revealing truth,
A rubber ducky claims my youth.

The quiet hides a joke or two,
As fish flash smiles while they swim through.
I watch the clouds all dressed in white,
Their shapes a circus, pure delight.

In this calm sea of jolly fun,
I grasp the sense of games begun.
Life's meaning flows in every cheer,
In laughter's arms, it all seems clear.

Beneath the Surface of Being

I once tried to find purpose,
But tripped over my own shoelace.
Fell face-first into the grass,
And asked if this was life's big race.

My cereal spilled in the morning,
Tiny flakes danced like they knew.
I wondered if they felt their calling,
Or just waited for someone to chew.

I climbed a tree for a new view,
Only to find squirrels debating.
The meaning of life, they concluded,
Was really just nuts for the taking.

In my bathtub, I ponder deep,
Rubber ducks float with profound pride.
Perhaps life's a splash or a leap,
Just hold on tight, enjoy the ride!

A Tale Woven in the Wind

Once I chased a butterfly,
Thinking it held secrets grand.
It landed on my sandwich, though,
And I just lost my lunch, unplanned!

Told my friends I'd find my groove,
So I joined a dance class, oh dear!
Tripped on my own two left feet,
They cheered while I expressed pure fear.

Riding bikes down silly hills,
Wind swept all my worries away.
Hit a bump, flew past my thrills,
And landed in a pile of hay!

A cat walked by, gave me a glare,
I'm certain it was judging me.
Perhaps the meaning's in the stare,
Or just seeing cats living free!

Fragments of a Soul's Quest

I once hiked a mountain high,
With snacks packed, I felt quite wise.
But the peak turned out to be fog,
And I lost my way to the skies.

My GPS led me astray,
To a spot with cows munching grass.
They mooed like they held deep truths,
But all I got was a big 'blagh!'

On a quest to find what's cool,
I tried meditating one fine day.
With my mind wandering to pizza,
I thought, "Maybe I should just play."

With every giggle and each grin,
Letting life's hiccups inspire.
I learned the secret underneath,
Is dancing while stuck in the mire!

The Lighthouses of Wisdom

I searched for wisdom near the shore,
In lighthouses both tall and bright.
But they just shined their big old beams,
While I struggled to find some light.

Tried asking a lighthouse keeper,
He only offered me a snack.
Said, "The meaning's in the cookies,"
Then promptly gave my brain a whack!

I built a sandcastle for answers,
But the tide thought it was a game.
It washed away my deep reflections,
And my structure was quite to blame.

So I danced with the waves at dusk,
Laughing hard at silly fate.
Perhaps life's more about the fun,
Than finding out what's truly great!

Spirits in the Weaving of Time

Time's a weaver with a grin,
Tying knots where we begin.
Rolling threads of joy and woes,
Laughing at where the fabric goes.

Every loop a silly jest,
Questions posed, and none addressed.
Colors clash, yet blend so fine,
Spirits clink in this yarn divine.

A tapestry of twists and bends,
Where sanity just twists and ends.
Finding joy in tangled thread,
To wear on days that feel like lead.

So here we are in threads so bright,
With spirits chatting day and night.
In this weave, just let it flow,
For life's a stitch, come join the show.

Radiance from Within

In the mirror, a face appears,
With toothpaste smudges and wild cheers.
Radiance glimmers from inside,
Like a disco ball on a fun ride.

Each laugh, a spark of silly light,
Reflecting back on silly plight.
Chasing dreams like running ants,
Overlooking life's quirky pants.

Folks search for gold in a big parade,
Yet miss the shoes that always played.
Finding brilliance in coffee stains,
And laughter that garners no refrains.

So shine your light, no need to hide,
Life's a stage, enjoy the slide.
With radiance spilling from your grin,
Embrace the joy that comes from within.

Paths Less Taken and Stories Untold

In the woods of choices wide,
I tripped on roots, with arms spread wide.
Paths less taken, got lost with glee,
Where squirrels plot their big marquee.

Stories untold, of coffee spills,
Of awkward chats and non-stop thrills.
Each wrong turn brings laughter's spark,
As we trip and fall in the dark.

Sidewalks paved with wobbly shoe,
Lead to places we never knew.
Adventures bloom like daisies bright,
Chasing cats in the moonlight.

So wander wide, and take your time,
With every silly step, a rhyme.
A tale unfolds in each misstep,
In the dance of paths, let's take the rep.

Dulcet Notes of Experience

Life's a cheeky little tune,
With melodies that swoon and croon.
Dulcet notes of joy and fuss,
Tickle my ears, and make a fuss.

Every bump like a boom bass drum,
Cymbals clash while I'm feeling numb.
A symphony of laughter's grace,
In crowded rooms, we find our place.

With every mishap, a giggling chord,
A melody strummed with no accord.
Playing tunes on pots and pans,
Composing life with silly plans.

So join the band, let's sing aloud,
In this peculiar, lovely crowd.
With dulcet notes, our hearts align,
Playing along, we're feeling fine.

Seeds of Knowledge Blooming

In a garden where wisdom grows,
Planting dreams in rows,
Watered by laughter and quirks,
We dig with joy, not much work.

With pearls of wisdom, we sow,
A few weeds, but oh, what a show,
Learning to dance with each new sprout,
Who knew knowledge could be so stout?

A sunflower nods, a smile wide,
With every stumble, we take in stride,
Chasing questions, oh, what a spree,
Who needs a map? Just giggle and see!

So sprinkle ideas like seeds so bright,
Watch them bloom with curious delight,
In this patch of life, let's give a cheer,
Growing up wise, year after year!

Flickers of Insight in the Dark

In the midst of night, a light so small,
A thought pops up, did you call?
Stumbling through shadows, tripping on dreams,
Finding truth in silly schemes.

A flashlight's beam, a goofy grin,
Makes the search for sense feel like a win,
Chasing reflections that dance and dart,
Who thought wisdom would tickle the heart?

Twinkling stars are just bright minds,
Whispering secrets of all kinds,
In the dark, we laugh at our fright,
Turning blunders into bright insight.

So when the night feels a bit absurd,
Remember the flickering joy you've heard,
Giggling paths lead to what's profound,
In the dark, funny truths abound!

Stones that Speak of History

Gather 'round, oh wise old stones,
With tales of laughter, not just groans,
They whisper secrets of ages past,
Of kings and jests, and shadows cast.

Each pebble knows how time can tease,
Worn by laughter, soaked in ease,
History's quirks etched with grace,
Stony faces with a cheeky face.

In crumbled ruins, echoes play,
Funny footnotes in yesterday,
Wit and wisdom, hand in hand,
Stones crack jokes about this land.

So listen close, let stories gleam,
As we unravel the quirky scheme,
With every laugh, we build a bridge,
From stone to stone, knowledge without a hitch!

Labyrinths of the Heart

In a maze of twists, lost we roam,
But wait! Is that a heart-shaped dome?
Getting tangled in emotion's flight,
Who knew love had such a funny bite?

With every turn, we laugh and tease,
Each corner turned brings both joy and ease,
A treasure map of quirky views,
Navigating ups and downs, what a ruse!

We stumble and trip, but with flair,
In this labyrinth, love fills the air,
Finding joy in each silly turn,
Wisdom grows from what we learn.

So dance through the paths, don't despair,
With giggles and grins, show you care,
In the heart's maze, let laughter prevail,
For the best maps are drawn in detail!

The Map of Infinite Roads

With a map that's upside down,
I wander without a frown.
Every turn is quite a jest,
Finding wrong paths is the best.

Directions given by my cat,
Insisted on a midnight chat.
They said, 'Just follow the moon's glow,'
But ended up in a burrito show.

A fork in the road, oh dear me,
One path led to a circus spree.
The other sold socks from a tent,
Guess which one I truly went!

In the end, I lost my shoe,
Found a goat that wanted stew.
Life's map has twists that tease,
And laughter flows just like the breeze.

Sunrise at Tomorrow's Horizon

Chasing sunsets with a kite,
I tripped and fell, oh what a sight!
The sun peeked up, laughed out loud,
While I tangled in my own cloud.

Coffee stains on my new shirt,
Swatted bugs and face-planted dirt.
The day starts fresh with a grin,
But somehow I'm still facing in.

I tried to catch the morning light,
But ended up in a pillow fight.
Feathers flying, a glorious sight,
Sunrise won, I'll nap tonight!

With each laugh, the dawn unfolds,
As dreams turn into playful golds.
Tomorrow's horizon sings to me,
Even in chaos, I feel free.

Underneath the Woven Sky

Under a sky with too many stars,
I strum my guitar, dreaming of cars.
Two squirrels formed a rock band there,
Jamming tunes without a care.

A shooting star offered a ride,
But I just waved it off with pride.
Who needs wishes when you've got snacks?
The universe grins as my patience cracks.

Clouds drift by like marshmallow boats,
They nudge each other, gossiping notes.
I shout, 'Hey, what's the scoop up high?'
They giggle softly, just passing by.

My blanket fort has the best views,
With a TV made of old shoes.
Underneath this cozy sky,
Life dances by, oh me, oh my!

Mutable Horizons

Horizons shift like gelatin molds,
One moment serious, next, it unfolds.
I tiptoe along, trying not to fall,
Hey, is that a pickle wearing a shawl?

Each step forward gives a squeak,
I ask a cactus, "What's the peak?"
He shrugs with arms that prick and poke,
Says, "Just run fast or get burnt toast."

Time wobbles on this silly path,
With every turn brings a new laugh.
A wise old tortoise tried to race,
But ended up in a silly place.

Mutable horizons full of tricks,
Life's a dance of clumsy flicks.
When meaning mixes with absurdity,
I giggle, thinking, "What a world to see!"

Navigating the Currents Within

I set my sails with quite the flair,
But the wind said, 'Not in my hair!'
I zigged and zagged like a loose kite,
Wondering if this was really my flight.

I tripped on rocks, lost my shoes,
Chased my thoughts like a confused moose.
Found a map drawn by a squirrel,
Which led to a land of pearls and twirls!

Through foggy days and sunlit beams,
I danced with shadows and chased bright dreams.
With laughter echoing in this quest,
I learned that life's simply a jest!

So if you wander and lose your way,
Just smile and dance, don't dismay.
For every detour and silly spree,
Is a chapter in your quirky spree!

A Canvas Painted with Experience

With colors bright, I grabbed my brush,
And painted chaos in a rush.
Purple skies and green sunflowers,
My masterpiece was made of hours.

I splashed my thoughts with glee and flair,
Only to find a cat sitting there.
He knocked my canvas, spilled the blue,
Yelled, 'You call this art? Oh if they knew!'

I grabbed some glitter, found a swirl,
The cat just blinked like, 'What a world!'
We mixed the odd with the next cliché,
Creating a scene that danced in dismay.

But in the mess, there's beauty true,
In every cringe and silly hue.
When life's colors run amok and blend,
Just smile and paint, that's the trend!

The Seasons of Self-Discovery

Spring dropped in with a vibrant cheer,
Asked if I had grown a beard yet, dear.
I said, 'No!' while searching for shoes,
And laughed at how life's full of clues.

Summer popped out with a sun-kissed grin,
Inviting me to join the spin.
I stumbled upon a field of bees,
Learning dances with hilarious ease.

Fall arrived on a skateboard thump,
With leaves that giggled, 'Come join the jump!'
I tripped and tumbled, sports I adore,
Finding joy in each silly score.

Winter came with a frosty wink,
Wrapped me tight like, 'Don't you stink?'
Through seasons odd and funny too,
I learned to smile with every view!

Finding Clarity in the Chaos

In the whirlwind of things, I lost my hat,
It spun around like a playful cat.
Chasing thoughts like it was a game,
Chaos giggled—life has no shame!

A sandwich fell while running in haste,
In my pocket was a half-eaten waste.
Laughter erupted, oh what a sight,
Was my lunch camping here for the night?

Then a notice popped by, loud and clear,
'Embrace the mess, let go of fear!'
So I danced through the clutter and clamor,
Finding joy in this silly glamour.

With every misstep and twist in fate,
I found my path in chaotic state.
And as I chuckled, I finally knew,
Life's clarity shines brightest when askew!

Sunsets and New Beginnings

Chasing sunsets that dance on the sea,
I tripped on my shoelace, oh woe is me!
With each stumble, I question the way,
Is wisdom found in such clumsy ballet?

Turning the pages of unwritten plans,
I asked a squirrel, who just shook his hands.
He told a joke, 'Why cross the road, friend?'
To find out if this is where the fun ends!

Laughing with shadows that stretch in the light,
I ponder my purpose, and sip on my Sprite.
Why search for the answer under the moon?
Maybe it's hidden in old cartoons!

So here's to the giggles, the gaffes, and the spry,
Learning life's secrets while bidding goodbye.
With sunset's last blush and a wink from the sky,
I embrace all the mess, and I float on my high!

The Pulse of the Open Road

Driving down highways with snacks by my side,
Every mile's an adventure, I take in my stride.
The GPS tells me, 'You are nearly there!'
But the map in my head leads me elsewhere!

I wave at the cows, they moo back with glee,
Not a care in the world; oh, what a sight to see!
A detour to nowhere, I laugh at the game,
Guess life's not a race; it's more like a fame!

Passing through towns with names I can't spell,
Each stop's a new story or a funny tale to tell.
Did the chicken cross just to baffle the car?
If only those feathers could take me far!

As the sun sets low in the rear-view mirror,
I realize my journey filled with humor is clear.
So I'll steer this old ride with laughter in sight,
For life's true meaning is found in delight!

A Fine Thread in the Fabric of Existence

Stitching my days with needle and thread,
Each laugh is a patch, and every tear shed.
With scissors in hand, I snip doubts a way,
Hoping my quilt will keep chaos at bay!

Fabric of life, with patterns so bold,
Some woven with joy, others frayed and old.
'Is that a glitch?' I can't help but muse,
Oh yes, it's my socks, they never do fuse!

Gathered around moments that sparkle and shine,
Sharing with friends, a glass (or two) of wine.
Threads intertwining, they laugh and they shout,
Who needs perfection when fun's all about?

So embrace every flaw, let life's fabric sway,
A tapestry rich, in its own quirky way.
With each bizarre patch, let the colors collide,
In the quilt of existence, let laughter be wide!

Embracing the Unwritten

In a book yet to write, I dance with delight,
Each word is a tickle, a laugh, pure light.
I pen silly stories, let my quirks unfold,
Who thought life's secrets are better than gold?

Pages turned gently with ink made of cheer,
Worrying less as I sip on my beer.
I scribble some nonsense, a rhyme or a jest,
Claiming this nonsense is truly the best!

With chapters uncertain, I jump and I twirl,
Finding the punchline in every big swirl.
If fate hands me lemons, I'll make jokes instead,
Juggling surprises in a circus ahead!

So here I stand, both a clown and a sage,
Painting my canvas, no need for a cage.
For in every blank space where laughter runs free,
I find all the things that are truly just me!

Barriers of Convention Broken

In a world of suits and ties,
I wore my pajamas to the prize,
They said, 'That's not how you win!',
I replied, 'Who said it's a sin?'

They told me to follow the line,
But my feet just wouldn't align,
With tick-tock rules they all held dear,
I danced like a weirdo, oh dear!

With hats of fruit and silly shoes,
Each oddity gave me the blues,
Yet with every chuckle I found,
The true treasures waiting around.

So here's to the barriers we shatter,
And all of the nonsense that mattered,
In chaos we're all set free,
Laughing all the way to our glee.

Dreams etched in the Sand

I drew my dreams on the beach sand,
A rocket ship, a big band,
The tide rolled in, made my hopes soak,
I shrugged and laughed, 'A silly joke!'

With castles high, my plans glowed bright,
But waves had other plans in sight,
The sandman laughed as my dreams fled,
I built a sandworm instead!

Each grain, a thought washed away,
Yet new ones came to play each day,
I pondered, 'What does it really mean?'
As I chased shells, following the gleam.

In the end, as the sunset unveiled,
I found joy in the dreams that sailed,
For life's a laugh, a sand dune dance,
A whimsical twist, a sandy romance.

Traces of the Unveiled Soul

In whispers, my soul took a stroll,
With mismatched socks, I lost control,
I spilled my thoughts like hot cocoa,
And giggled at all my inner woe.

Each truth revealed like a magic trick,
The audience laughed as I lost my pick,
From fears to dreams, I let them flow,
In the circus of life, I'm the star of the show.

Dancing around my quirks like a fool,
Finding wisdom in a wacky school,
With lessons learned on muffin tops,
Every stumble led to more fun stops.

So here's to the traces we leave behind,
In laughter, our secrets we find,
With every giggle and playful swoon,
The unveiled soul howls at the moon.

Inked in the Pages of Time

In a library filled with dusty tales,
I trip on a book, it never fails.
A map of my life, or so it seems,
Turns out it's just a book of ice cream dreams.

I wander through stories of brave knights,
Yet here I am, in my pajamas, no fights.
Swinging on chandeliers made of light,
My heart wears a crown, but the head feels slight.

Every tome holds secrets, both wise and strange,
Like finding a sock that's been lost in the range.
I laugh at the lessons the pages spill,
Life's recipe seems to be overcooked thrill.

Inked in the margins, a note so clear,
"Next time, stop asking, just grab a beer."
So I flip the pages, from front to back,
With laughter and whimsy, I keep on track.

Labyrinth of Yearnings

In a maze full of choices, I zig and I zag,
Hoping one path will gift me a brag.
But every time I think I've got it, oh dear,
I end up with a sandwich and a cold fizzy beer.

The map's upside down, or am I just lost?
I chase after dreams, not counting the cost.
Each turn leads to giggles, a tumble and roll,
Like a jester on stilts losing his soul.

I thought I'd seek wisdom, profound and grand,
Instead I found clowns in a one-man band.
They dance all around with pies and confetti,
Teaching me laughter when life's not so petty.

With every corner turned, I see folks just grin,
Their smiles the compass guiding me in.
So I skip through the maze, embrace every whim,
For joy is the treasure, not stuffy or dim.

Whispers of the Wandering Soul

A soul on the prowl, what can it find?
Echoes of laughter are not so unkind.
I dance with my shadows, let out a squeal,
   For each step I take is a zany reveal.

Whispers of wisdom float through the air,
Tell me to chill, and to not have a care.
With every misstep, a chuckle I earn,
In this game of life, it's my turn to learn.

The compass is broken, but hey, that's just fine,
I'll follow the ducks, maybe sip some wine.
With each silly stumble, I gather my cheer,
Life's meaning is wrapped in a light-hearted leer.

So here's to the wanderers, lost and bemused,
We wear our confusion, never bruised.
With laughter the guide, I'll roam and I'll glide,
In whispers of joy, I'll always abide.

Mosaic of Moments

In a patchwork of time, I stitch and I sew,
Moments like buttons in a colorful row.
Some days are shiny, others a mess,
Like a cat in a hat, oh, what a distress!

Each second a bead, I string them with care,
Bright reds and blues floating through the air.
I try to be deep, but I trip on my lace,
And find joy in chaos, life's fast-paced race.

A sprinkle of laughter, a dash of surprise,
Like a chef who forgets what spice to advise.
Through blunders and giggles, I gather my quilt,
In this tapestry woven, my worries are spilt.

So here's to the jigsaw, the wild, the free,
Each piece fits together, just let it be.
In a mosaic of moments, I make my own song,
Embracing the silly, where I truly belong.

Remnants of Roadside Revelations

Bumping along in a rickety car,
With snacks exploding from a jar.
A flat tire is more than a fuss,
It's an excuse to discover the bus.

The maps are such ancient displays,
We're lost in a digital maze.
"Turn left at the giant rock," you say,
I think it's a creature that doesn't play!

Sipping coffee from a dog-shaped mug,
Life's mysteries unraveled with a shrug.
When did we ditch our grand routine?
For a detour that's downright obscene?

The sun sets over snappy cafés,
We chuckle at life in ridiculous ways.
In faded pubs, we find our cheer,
Who knew wisdom lurked near cold beer?

Conversations with the Wind

The breeze whispers tales from afar,
I shout back, "You're a bizarre star!"
Tickling my hat, it gives me a tease,
As if we're both free to do as we please.

"Hey, Wind, what's the point of this race?"
"It's to dance, my friend, not just chase."
With every gust, I cannot resist,
An impromptu tango, we jump and twist.

Clouds eavesdrop on our silly chat,
I tell them my dreams with a soft pat.
They rain with laughter, then float away,
While I chase squirrels to brighten my day.

Twists and turns, the forecast is strange,
Yet with each gust, I feel such a change.
Life's made for laughter, not just the grind,
Thanks, dear Wind, for your funny mind!

The Alchemy of Adventures

Mixing laughter with a pinch of fear,
Stirred with a dash of a crazy idea.
We've turned socks into treasure maps,
And wardrobe doors into reality gaps.

In one corner, a garden gnome stands,
Claiming lands with ridiculous demands.
He sells magic beans, flowering dreams,
While I sip tea from a shoe, or so it seems.

Let's forge new paths with glittery ropes,
While plotting secret plans with our hopes.
Even a sandwich can be a quest,
When you're splitting crumbs on a wild fest.

With each mishap, we gather our charms,
A parade of quirks and elbow-bumps warms.
So here's to adventures in mismatched shoes,
Because life's laughter is the best muse!

Raindrops on an Open Mind

Pitter-patter on rooftops of dreams,
Each drop a giggle in silvery beams.
Umbrellas flip in a ludicrous dance,
Like clumsy penguins caught in a trance.

I walk through puddles with my best mate,
Splashing away all doubts and fate.
"Why so serious?" I ask a wet cat,
He replies, "I'm judging your hat!"

As clouds roll in, we conjure a scheme,
To catch rainbows, or so it would seem.
Our laughter grows, it fills the rain,
Taking life lightly, forgetting the pain.

So let's twirl in the showers today,
And whistle tunes in a silly way.
For each raindrop falls with giggly flair,
Teaching us joy is found everywhere!

The Compass of Introspection

Upon my desk, a compass spun,
Pointing to snacks, oh what fun!
I ponder life with every bite,
Is pizza a path, or sheer delight?

I scribble thoughts, with much dismay,
In search of wisdom, I start to sway.
But where's the map for souls like me?
Just Google it—oh, that's the key!

Through tangled thoughts, my pencil flies,
Attempting to follow some wise guy's ties.
Yet the only route that feels so bright,
Is one that ends with cake tonight!

So here I sit, a traveler bold,
With stories of pastries and mysteries told.
If life's a road, I'll take the detour,
For cookies and laughs, that's for sure!

Beneath the Canopy of Questions

Under the trees, where squirrels scamper,
I question life, but bring no answer.
"What's the point?" I ask the leaves,
They rustle back, like little thieves.

The sun peeks through, a shining scout,
Chasing bugs, as I wander about.
Do I need a guide or a magic map?
Or just a nap on a fluffy lap?

Owls hoot wisdom, or so they say,
But all I hear is 'get out and play!'
If the tree of truth is tall and grand,
Why can't I snack while making a stand?

I pirouette with questions galore,
Spinning 'round, seeking something more.
But in the chaos, I realize this—
Life's meaning might just taste like bliss!

Sunrise Over Uncharted Waters

Morning breaks with a splash of sound,
Sunrise paints the sky all around.
Where to go? The seas are wide,
I'll ask a seagull—what a guide!

My boat's afloat, but so is foam,
Navigating waves, I feel at home.
With coffee in hand, I shout, "Ahoy!"
May I find treasure—or just a toy?

Fish swim by, wearing tiny hats,
They wink at me, oh cheeky brats!
Life's essence floats like driftwood dreams,
Or maybe it's lost in my ice cream seams!

As I zigzag on this endless spree,
I ponder if the sea ponders me.
But laughter echoes on this quest,
And maybe fun is life's true zest!

Seeking the Heart's Horizon

With binoculars in hand, I peer,
Searching horizons, full of cheer.
Is that a dream on the skyline bright?
Or just a mirage—last night's delight?

I tripped over thoughts, no footpath clear,
Discouraged a bit, I shed a tear.
But wait! Is that a taco stand?
Yes, my compass swings to food so grand!

I chase the horizon with a cheesy grin,
Behind every cloud lies sweet cinnamon.
To find the meaning, must I race?
Naw, I stop for cake—it's all about pace!

As I roam, those questions arise,
Does the heart hum loud or merely sigh?
But then I laugh; with every bite,
I find life's meaning—what a delight!

The Pilgrim's Silent Watch

With a backpack stuffed, I stroll so slow,
The map's upside down, where should I go?
I ask a chicken, it just squawks back,
Now I'm left wondering, did I lose the track?

Mountains high and valleys deep,
Tired feet, but not a peep.
I trip on roots and faceplant mud,
Life's a dance, and I'm a dud!

I meet a squirrel, we share a snack,
He gives me wisdom - "Don't look back!"
With each misstep, I laugh and cheer,
Turns out the path was always here!

So here I stand at the end of day,
Chasing meaning, come what may.
A pilgrimage of giggles and grins,
Who knew this quest could lead to wins?

Moments Carved in Time

I sit on a bench, a hot dog in hand,
Life's mysteries unfold, just as I planned.
A bird drops a gift—oh, what a surprise!
Laughter erupts as I wipe my eyes.

While folks rush by, I take a seat,
One thought strikes me—oh, the world's a treat!
I juggle my nachos, fumble and sway,
Is this the time that's worth the play?

Sunsets linger like last week's pie,
I muse and munch as the colors fly.
A child yells, "Look! I can fly, I swear!"
As I ponder meaning, I spill my fare.

Moments are like these, messy yet grand,
Meaning's a hot dog—not just a plan.
So here's to mishaps, and laughter divine,
With mustard and ketchup, life's treats intertwine!

Footfalls on Ancient Paths

On ancient paths where legends tread,
I slip on moss, bump my head.
A wise old tree leans down to say,
"Do you need help? Or just a play?"

Footprints wander, these shoes are tight,
Every twist and turn feels just right.
I chase a lizard, he zigzags away,
He must be thinking, is this a game?

I found an arrow, old and bent,
Could it lead to gold? Or just a dent?
With each poky stick and bump on the track,
I wave at the clouds as they laugh at my back.

With giggles aplenty, and snacks to share,
I dance with shadows without a care.
Footfalls echo, but joy's the prize,
Maybe the meaning's just in the skies!

A Portrait of Perseverance

With paintbrush poised, I start to explore,
What is perseverance? I'm not sure!
I smudge some green, then splash on blue,
Oops! The cat's now an abstract too!

Telling tales of trips taken wide,
With spilled coffee as my trusty guide.
A canvas scrambles, colors collide,
They dance and tumble, nowhere to hide!

Brushes grow weary, my hands a mess,
Is it perseverance, or pure distress?
A masterpiece bubbling with chaotic glee,
"Art is just life," I hear from the bee.

In each silly stroke, I vibrantly seek,
What makes life meaningful? Laughs, not bleak!
So I greet my canvas, all wild and loud,
In this funny portrait, I'm wholly proud!

Treading Between Dreams

With mismatched shoes I start my quest,
In search of wisdom, not the best!
A map of jellybeans in my hand,
I dance with squirrels, life is grand!

I chased a butterfly; it led me wrong,
Through fields of laughter, I sang my song.
A talking tree gave me some advice,
"Play hopscotch with clouds, it's quite nice!"

I stumbled upon a laughing brook,
It told me stories, I stopped to look.
With giggles echoing all around,
I found my direction without a sound!

In my dreams, I flipped and flew,
Tripped on rainbows, found a clue.
Though not about meaning, fun's the key,
Life's silly antics have set me free!

Compass of the Heart

With my heart acting as a compass, bright,
I ventured forth, full of delight.
Yet every turn felt a bit bizarre,
Like following a llama in a car!

I sailed on pancakes, syrup for fuel,
Waved to a zebra who played it cool.
'You'll find your path,' it said while munching,
The maps made of candy were quite ungodly crunching!

A hula-hooping turtle, quite a sight,
Taught me to dance with sheer delight.
In circles I spun, lost in the jest,
My quest grew foamy, but I felt blessed!

So when the sun set, casting its glow,
I realized that it's all about the show.
A veritable circus served me my part,
Each laugh a needle, stitching my heart!

Unraveled by Stars

I looked for answers in the night sky,
But found a raccoon who asked me why.
With twinkling eyes, it stole my snacks,
I laughed hard, not looking back!

The constellations played a game of hide,
While I pondered my purpose with a peanut pie.
Saturn winked, Mars did a jig,
Life's deep meaning seemed quite big!

Then a comet zoomed, asking me to race,
'Can finding oneself include some space?'
I zoomed too fast, crash-landed on grass,
The next stop was a thoughtful rhino's class!

So here I am, with stars all around,
Not much wisdom, but laughter I've found.
In the cosmos, where dreams collide,
Funny moments spark joy inside!

Navigating Through Time

With a clock as my GPS, I took a leap,
My time-traveling toaster beeped, beeped!
I landed in the past just in time,
To see a dinosaur attempting to rhyme.

I asked, 'Hey buddy, what's your scene?'
He said, 'Just chilling, living the dream!'
Together we danced on a giant slice of pie,
Time doesn't matter when you're that high!

From ancient lands to futuristic sights,
I dodged robots with glittering lights.
While navigating years with a wiggle and twist,
I learned that laughter's the plot you can't miss!

So here I stand, with time on my side,
Waving at moments as they glide.
In this wacky time chase and glee,
I found fun's the essence, that's key, you see!

Reflections on a Pebbled Shore

A pebble tossed, it skips with glee,
A fishy friend shouts, "Look at me!"
The seagulls cackle, making a fuss,
While I ponder life, lost in the struss.

The waves dance in a quirky mime,
Time's a joker, always a crime.
I trip on shells, it's quite a sight,
Life's puzzle pieces, oh what a plight!

Collecting thoughts like shells so rare,
Each one a story, oh if you dare!
A crab sneaks by with a sideways glance,
"Finding wisdom? It's just chance!"

So here I stand, on this sandy floor,
With giggles echoing, I want more!
The tide brings laughs along with woes,
And life's big meaning? Who really knows!

Pillars of Wisdom Under the Sky

Beneath the clouds, I question fate,
An owl hoots, "Life's never late!"
I ask a squirrel for sage advice,
He scurries off, that cheeky slice!

Old trees stand in their leafy suits,
While squirrels hold high their festive boots.
"Dance with the breeze," they whisper and grin,
While the rocks just sit, tight-lipped within.

A turtle winks, says, "Take it slow,
Chase after meaning? Where'd it go?"
I trip on roots, stumble through thought,
The forest giggles—what have I sought?

With every whisper of rustling leaves,
I chalk it up; life's a game of eves.
And though I stand with questions nigh,
I chuckle loud under this vast sky.

A Cartographer's Heart

Maps in hand, I wander wide,
Each twist and turn: a wild ride.
"I lost my way!" for laughs I scoff,
Directions? Who needs them? Let's just scoff!

An X marks spots of fleeting mirth,
I chart my laughs, it's my true worth.
A compass spins; it makes no sense,
Perhaps I should consult my cat's immense.

With dotted lines of dreams untold,
I scribble thoughts, my heart's bold.
"Here's a treasure!" says the sneaky crow,
"Just open your eyes, let wisdom flow!"

Adventuring forth with a giggle or two,
I'll map all my blunders, they're fun, it's true!
For meaning found isn't a straight line,
It's a cartographer's joy, sparkling like wine!

Banners of Belief Waving High

In the land of dreams, I raise my flag,
A unicorn prances, no need to brag.
I wave my banner with giddy delight,
"Who needs rules? Let's take flight!"

With beliefs that wobble like jelly on toast,
I toast the silly, they matter most.
Each laugh is a flag, colors bright,
A parade of ideas in sunlight's bite.

A wise old frog croaks from the mire,
"Hold on to joy, that's the real fire!"
I trip on a joke, slip on a pun,
With each silly thought, life's just begun.

So here we raise our quirky flags,
Amidst giggles, snorts, and cheerful jags.
And as we dance with our banners wide,
Meaning springs from this whimsical ride!

Footprints on the Road Less Traveled

I walked a path of prickly thorns,
Dodging life like a cat with scorns.
Found a funny hat on the way,
Wore it proud – a bright display.

A squirrel winked, or so I thought,
His judgment made me feel distraught.
But then he danced on a little log,
Turning my woes to a merry jog.

I tripped on roots, did a clumsy twist,
Made new friends – I couldn't resist.
We laughed at all the silly falls,
A party of mishaps, after all!

So here I am with shoes untied,
Chasing clouds, my silly guide.
Life's all about the quirky ride,
With laughter as my trusted stride.

Searching for the Quiet Truth

In a library of loud thoughts,
I searched for peace among the plots.
A book fell down with a great big thud,
I laughed aloud at the dusty dud.

The cat nearby just gave a glare,
As if to say, 'Life's not fair!'
I offered him my half-eaten snack,
He turned away, I felt the lack.

I pondered life like a curious bee,
Buzzing 'round, attempting to see.
But all I found were silly rhymes,
Stuck in my head like jumbled crimes.

Then came a dog, with a wagging tail,
He seemed to know life's simple trail.
Together we chased our lost thoughts,
In the chaos, a quiet truth we sought.

Maps Made of Memories

I drew a map with crayons bright,
Tracing paths both wild and light.
With mountains of cheese and rivers of jam,
It looked like a feast, oh what a sham!

The X marks where I lost my shoe,
A treasure found in a field of dew.
Dragons made of flowers guarded the way,
Barking warnings in their floral ballet.

As I ventured, with giggles and glee,
Each step led to a new memory.
A picnic here, a dance in the rain,
A folder of laughter, the best of gain!

So if you ask where I've been all along,
I'll hand you my map, and maybe a song.
For life is a puzzle, a colorful maze,
Filled with chuckles and silly phase.

In Search of Golden Horizons

I set out to find those shining rays,
With a sandwich in hand for all my days.
The horizon giggled, 'Catch me if you can!'
I chased a mirage that looked like a fan.

Clouds shaped like bunnies floated above,
Each one whispering secrets of love.
But the sun just rolled its fiery eyes,
As I stumbled and tripped, oh what a surprise!

I found a wise turtle, moving so slow,
With jokes so corny, they made me glow.
'Patience, my friend, it's not a race,'
He chuckled and gifted me his warm embrace.

So I danced with shadows, laughed with the breeze,
On this quest for gold, I found sweet ease.
Life's a crazy ride, full of twists and turns,
In seeking the light, oh how my heart yearns!

The Unfolding of Self

I woke up one day with a sock on my foot,
Wondering if there's more than just breakfast and loot.
A mirror reflected a face full of cream,
Perhaps life's a joke, or maybe a dream.

I searched for my purpose under the bed,
Counted missing change and thoughts in my head.
Found my cat laughing, she seemed quite aware,
While I'm still confused with my unkempt hair.

I chased my own shadow around in a twirl,
And bumped into grasshoppers giving a whirl.
They chirped, "Keep dancing, you silly old chap,
The meaning of life might be a good nap!"

So I laid on the grass, sun shining so bright,
With questions and giggles until the moonlight.
If figuring it out means wearing two shoes,
I'll just keep on laughing, I've nothing to lose.

Across the Bridge of Time

I took a stroll down a bridge made of cheese,
Thought time would flow like a gentle breeze.
Instead, it melted; it stuck to my toes,
And pigeons stared down at my silly woes.

With each step I took, I tripped on my thoughts,
And pondered if wisdom was just tied in knots.
A squirrel ran by, accosting my mind,
"Life's just a game, leave the stress behind!"

Onward I traveled, through decades of fluff,
I found myself giggling, "This all feels quite tough!"
And when I tripped once more, what did I find?
A lost rubber duck with deep thoughts in mind.

I asked it the question, "Oh, what should I be?"
It quacked back with laughter, "Just be silly and free!"
So I tossed it aside, into a nearby stream,
Laughing aloud, "Yeah, life's not as it seems!"

Murmurs of the Universe

In the middle of night, I heard a soft hum,
Checked my fridge first, thought maybe it's them.
But it was just stars, in a cosmic parade,
Whispering secrets while I sat quite dismayed.

They giggled and twinkled, doing a jig,
And one shouted out, "Oh, don't be so big!
Life is but laughter, a pun or two,
Just don't ask the moon why it's feeling blue!"

I tried to eavesdrop on galaxies wide,
But they were too busy with their stellar ride.
While planets were arguing, which one's the best,
I just sipped some coffee, and wished them good rest.

So I lifted my chin, with a smile quite wide,
And joined in their chaos, enjoying the ride.
"Look at me, universe, I'm part of your dance!
Let's sprinkle some humor, and give life a chance!"

The Dance of Questions

Swung in my chair, with a book in my hand,
Questions were swirling, like dust in the sand.
"What's the meaning of life?" I pondered anew,
And tripped on my thoughts like a quirky ol' shoe.

They danced in a circle, all jumbled and bright,
One screamed out, "Turn left!" while another called, "Right!"
A parade of queries, all dressed up to play,
They twirled and they leaped, leading me astray.

So I joined in their frolic, with giggles galore,
Not knowing the answers, just wanting some more.
"Is it pizza or tacos that make us feel whole?"
They whispered, "It's joy, silly! Now let's rock 'n' roll!"

I found truth in laughter, that tickled my soul,
In questions and silliness, I felt quite whole.
So I danced with my queries, twirling all night,
Life's mysteries unsolved, but my heart felt just right.

Footprints on the Path of Dreams

I wandered down the road of fate,
With socks that never quite matched straight.
Each step a stumble, a giggle or two,
The path was muddy, but dreams were new.

Invisible gnomes laughed at my plight,
Chasing butterflies by the pale moonlight.
With every twist, a random surprise,
I found a treasure map in my fries.

A slip on a banana peel, oh what fun!
Sailed through puddles like I was the one.
With each goofy turn, I wore a big grin,
Learning through laughter, that's how I win.

So let's dance through life without a care,
With silly hats and mismatched flair.
For every misstep, there's joy to gleam,
On this wacky path where laughter reigns supreme.

Echoes in the Silent Forest

In a forest where the owls debate,
The trees wore hats, it seemed like fate.
I tried to listen, but the squirrels were loud,
Holding meetings, all huddled and proud.

I asked a raccoon, "What's life all about?"
He shrugged his furry shoulders and shouted, "No doubt!
It's all about munching on the finest snacks,
And making friends while avoiding the hacks!"

The path through the woods was a maze and a laugh,
With singing flowers, and a dancing giraffe.
We'd skip along like we knew what was right,
In a world full of chaos, we'd dance through the night.

So if you get lost in the silence and green,
Just follow the giggles where happiness is seen.
For in these wild woods, the meaning's not clear,
But laughter and joy are always so near.

Radiance Through the Fog

Through the fog, I waved to a cloud,
It waved back, it was feeling quite proud.
I searched for meaning, but tripped on my shoes,
And spilled my coffee, all over the news.

The sun peeked out, wearing a funny grin,
Shining bright, it said, "Let the fun begin!"
With joy in my heart, I jumped through the mist,
Chasing the giggles, no moment was missed.

I asked a shadow what life was to be,
It shrugged like a champ, "Just follow me!"
With every step, the fog turned to cheer,
I found my lost socks, but still not my beer.

When life gets cloudy, just dance in the haze,
With silly quirks and whimsical ways.
For through every struggle and misty night,
Laughter can turn the wrong into right.

Beyond Each Winding Road

I took a drive down a bumpy lane,
With my cat at the wheel, it drove me insane.
We laughed at the ducks that danced in a line,
Waving their wings, in a party divine.

Each curve brought a sign I could barely read,
"U-Turn Ahead!" or "Feed the Shetland Steed!"
With every corner, my worries flew far,
Even the GPS said, "You're a star!"

A flat tire led to a picnic in grass,
I tried to fix it, but only made it pass.
With sandwiches stored in the trunk for a feast,
We laughed till we cried, not bothered in the least.

So here's to the roads that twist and confound,
With laughter and love, the best life is found.
For every adventure, each bump, joyful ode,
Reveals the sweet meaning beyond each winding road.

Rivers of Remembrance

I paddled down a slippery stream,
With rubber ducks and a bubble dream.
Forgot my snacks, just chips have I,
A feast for squirrels as they scurry by.

With every splash, a memory flies,
Like fish in hats, beneath the skies.
I laugh at how I lost my way,
Chasing shadows into the fray.

My oar's a spoon, my boat a chair,
I paddle with flair, not really a care.
The current pulls but I just glide,
Trusting whimsy as my guide.

So here's to rivers, wacky and bright,
Where wrong turns lead to pure delight.
When all seems lost, I grinningly find,
Life's meaning is just a joke unkind.

The Art of Rediscovery

I found my socks beneath the bed,
An artful mess, I'd rather shred.
Old books and maps, I trip and fall,
Yet, laughter echoes down the hall.

With paint-stained hands, I craft and mold,
Sculpting laughter in colors bold.
My muse is coffee, a mix of roast,
I chuckle at what I love the most.

In rummaged treasures, I start anew,
A rubber chicken, yes, that'll do!
Embracing chaos, I spin and twirl,
Life's a carnival in a whirly swirl.

I paint my dreams on bathroom tiles,
Chasing purpose through silly smiles.
Every mishap gives me a grin,
In the art of life, I always win!

As the Leaves Whisper Tales

The leaves are gossiping, can you hear?
They talk of squirrels and my lost beer.
With every rustle, a tale unfolds,
About a naked tree that never grows old.

I ask them secrets, they laugh and spin,
Pointing at the gardener, a messy grin.
With laughter, autumn dances around,
As I trip over roots, grace unbound.

In swirling colors, they swish and sway,
Telling stories of bright, silly days.
Finding meaning in rustles and flips,
I discover truth, wrapped in leaf tips.

So here's to the leaves, wild and free,
Whispering secrets of what could be.
In laughter, I find my heart's tune,
Life's a leaf, floating under the moon.

In Search of Kindred Spirits

I wandered through a maze of cheese,
Searching for friends who'd share some peas.
With every corner, a wild surprise,
A clam in glasses, oh how he flies!

I asked a pickle, 'What should I be?'
He said, 'Try limbo, it's easy, you see!'
Fell on my face, but laughed till I cried,
In this quirky world, happiness abides.

A hopscotch turtle on skates rides by,
Twirling around like he's going to fly.
In the crowd of the odd, I found my place,
Smiling at everything, like it's a race.

So here's to the spirits, both silly and bright,
Who make life a circus, a delightful flight.
With each odd encounter, I learn to sing,
Meaning blooms in laughter, oh what joy it can bring!

Reflections in Still Waters

In a pond, I saw my face,
Screaming back, what a disgrace!
Thought I'd ponder deep and wise,
But it's just ducks that caught my eyes.

Life's a riddle, don't you see?
Found my socks, just lost a key.
Should I wander or should I run?
Is this a crisis, or just fun?

Chasing the Horizon's Call

Horizon winks, it's such a tease,
I run to catch it, skinned my knees.
There's a rainbow, oh so bright,
But it's just an ice cream cart in sight.

With a cone in hand, I start to sing,
Life's absurd, it's a silly thing.
Chasing dreams like kids with kites,
While juggling snacks and planning bites.

Blossoms of Discovery

In the garden, I plant my thoughts,
With a trowel and a pair of shorts.
Sunflowers laugh, they tilt their heads,
While I trip over my own two threads.

Each bloom a question, bright and bold,
Why are socks so hard to fold?
Nature giggles, wisdom blooms,
As I dig through my own old dooms.

Beyond the Edge of Comfort

Step outside my cozy nest,
Get attacked by bugs, I jest.
A new café, it's quite a fright,
With herbal tea that tastes just right.

Pushed past limits, what a thrill,
With every sip, I get a chill.
Embracing chaos, what a mess,
Life's a circus, I must confess.

Chasing Shadows

I chased a shadow on my street,
With sneakers on, I felt so fleet.
It turned a corner, quick and sly,
And here I am, just passing by.

The shadow laughed, it looked so sleek,
I shouted, "Come!" but it won't speak.
We played tag with the sunny rays,
And lost the game in so many ways.

A chicken joined and ran amok,
Said, "What's the fuss? You'll never clock!"
But with my trusty rubber duck,
I brought it home, now that's just luck.

So here I sit on this warm bench,
Eating snacks that smell like wrench.
If meaning hides in shadow's dance,
I'll catch it yet, just give me a chance.

Embracing Light

I danced with light, it twinkled bright,
Like fireflies in the warm night.
I tripped on rays, fell on my face,
Did the moon laugh? I lost my grace!

A cat jumped in, with sass and flair,
It said, "You ought to get some air!"
We vibed together, just two fools,
In search of wisdom, breaking rules.

The sun then blinked, a winking star,
Said, "Find your path, don't stray too far!"
With shades on, I looked cool as ice,
"Existence is just pizza, slice by slice!"

So off I went, in this bright space,
Ready to meet each cheeky face.
If life's a joke, with puns and might,
I'll laugh along, embracing light.

Reflections in the River of Time

I peered into a bubbling stream,
Saw my face and jumped, oh dream!
Time winked back, like a playful sprite,
"Just keep swimming! Don't lose sight!"

I caught a fish wearing a tie,
It asked, "What's up?" I said, "Oh my!"
We discussed the best flavors of pie,
As clouds formed shapes that made me sigh.

A duck paddled by in a grand parade,
"Lost in thought? Come join the charade!"
With water wings and a funky hat,
We laughed at time, like a silly chat.

So splash I will in this playful flow,
Each giggle echoed, soft and low.
If life's a pool with ripples and rhyme,
Then let's make waves in our river of time.

Bridges Built on Understanding

I built a bridge with gummy stacks,
It wobbled hard, then fell with cracks.
But squirrels applauded with acorn cheer,
And if they loved it, who needs fear?

I crossed the bridge with a jellybean,
Proclaimed, "This place is quite the scene!"
Then tripped on laughter, fell in a heap,
Found hidden truths in a jellybean heap.

A wise old tree gave advice so nice,
"To understand, just ask once or twice!"
So with a grin, I took a leap,
Into conversations, my heart to keep.

With marshmallow friends and a gummy crew,
We danced across with a joyful view.
In this sweet realm, I feel so grand,
Understanding flows like sugar in hand.

The Quest for Lost Colors

I searched for colors in a dull gray town,
Where pastels crept in, oh what a frown!
A rainbow whispered, "Don't be shy!"
So off I went, determined to fly.

I met a crayon with a crooked smile,
"Lost my glory for quite a while!"
We painted walls with orange dreams,
And watched as laughter flowed in streams.

A polka-dotted dog joined the ride,
"Colors are wild! Come take my side!"
We splashed cerulean, fuchsia, and lime,
Creating a storm in a long-lost rhyme.

So here I am in this colorful race,
Finding joy in every silly place.
If meaning hides in the hues I see,
I'll blend them all, just let them be.

www.ingramcontent.com/pod-product-compliance
Lightning Source LLC
Chambersburg PA
CBHW051633160426
43209CB00004B/630